Riddle of Life

Cuffee the Magnificent

DEDICATION

Mom & Dad

DEDICATION

CONTENTS

ACKNOWLEDGMENTS

I thank God for giving me a spirit of creativity.

I thank my family and friends for their encouragement.

I thank you, the reader, for supporting my work.

SORROW

I am standing here in the desert alone

There is no one

No one

Around

The only thing I can think to do

Is to walk forward

To try to find answers

Because I need answers

I want answers

I want to understand how I got here

I want to understand how I can leave here

I remember being in water

And rising up from a pool

A river

A lake

And taking a breath

Taking in life

And singing joyful joyful

Understanding light

But from that moment till now

It's all erased

And all I can remember

Is waking up here

In this cold

Dry

Dark

Desert

What will I do?

Where will I go?

SUFFERING

Someone help me

Will someone rescue me?

A helicopter

A plane

A tank

A jeep

Will there be anyone

To save me

To be a redeemer on a tree

For me will there be?

Or will I sit here

Hidden between two rocks?

Will I sit here

Freezing

Hungry

Alone?

SONG OF LIFE

Then I heard
In the distance
Someone say
"Sing a Song of Life!"

I looked
And it was a man
Waving his hands
To get my attention

He was up on the hill
Near the horizon
And he said again
"Sing a Song of Life"

But I did not understand

I'm cold

I'm thirsty

I'm hungry

Do you understand?

I am sick

I am tired

I am worn

How can I sing a Song of Life

When all I have is dying?

The man ran to me

With all his speed

The last sprint of a marathon

To run swiftly as he could

As if to rescue someone from drowning

As if to save a child from danger

FOUNTAIN

He huddled beside me

Placed his hand on my shoulder

And he said

"You might be cold

You might be lost

But you are not alone

There are more for you

Than you see"

I said to him

"But how can I sing a Song of Life

When there is no life in me

All I have are questions

Questions with no answers"

He said to me

"You look to the north

You look to the south

You look to the east

And you look to the west

You try to see with your two eyes

And you try to hear with your two ears

And you try to understand the world"

He stood to his feet and exclaimed

"But this is where you fall short!

Because your eyes deceive you!

Your ears play a trick on you!"

On one knee and with stretched out hand

"But if you shut your eyes

And close your ears

If you mute your voice

And touch no object

Open your heart

And receive from within

And a fountain

Of Infinite

Eternal

Depth

Will arise"

I asked,

"Is this the Song of Life

That you want me to sing?"

HOME

The man grabbed my arm

Pulled me up to my feet

He said

"Let's leave this place

Let's leave this desert

Follow me up that hill!

Have you ever been

On the other side of that hill?

Do you know what's over there?"

I answered

"No

I don't know what's beyond that hill

Or any other hill

I don't know what's beyond this desert

All I remember is being in the water
And bursting forth from it
Taking a breath
Then I was here"

He said as he pulled me toward the hill
"If that's all you know
Then there is much to receive"

Step by step we took
Faster ever still
Closer and closer we were
Nearer to that hill

At the base of its foot
We stood at every stand
Look to the hills
Where does your help come from?

Whatever we find beyond this land

To the top ever knowing

With every ascent

With my life ever showing

A piece

A part

Until a promised land appeared

Not desert

Not cold

Not dark

It was a square

A plot of land

Lush with vegetation

And with life

"What is that place?"

I asked

And he said

"Home"

DESIRE

We came to the border

At the foot of the other side

It was the line that separated

The grassy field

From the dry desert

We stood at that border

At that gateway

At that shore

I asked

"Is there anything I need to do?

Is there some type of ritual I need to perform?

This place you call Home

Seems so sacred that I need to

Do something to make myself presentable

The man said softly,

"No

All you need to do is cross over

Into the square

Into the grassy land

And Home will make you"

So together

With our left

We stepped into the grassy land

Then with our right

We stood

Home

Immediately

I felt

All the questions I had before were irrelevant

Everything that I thought was important

Wasn't important anymore

I didn't need to know how I got to the desert

It wasn't important for me to understand

The extent of my make up

I didn't need to know

Or even have a desire or longing

For facts and figures

That did not apply

To home

To wholeness

To a whole life

I don't know everything

I don't understand everything

But that's all right

Because I'm Home

It's okay

That everything is not in my grasp

Because I am finally

Home

ABOUT THE AUTHOR

Cuffee the Magnificent is a musician and poet that ignites a passion for life and truth in the hearts of audiences around the world.

www.CuffeeMagnificent.com

ADDITIONAL WORKS

Poetry

Doxology of Nonlocality

Music

Riddle of Life
A Musical Interpretation

Doxology of Nonlocality
A Musical Interpretation

www.ingramcontent.com/pod-product-compliance
Lightning Source LLC
Chambersburg PA
CBHW030012040426
42337CB00012BA/757